WHATAMELON

An Hachette UK Company
www.hachette.co.uk

First published in Great Britain in 2019 by Pyramid,
an imprint of Octopus Publishing Group Ltd
Carmelite House, 50 Victoria Embankment,
London EC4Y 0DZ
www.octopusbooks.co.uk

ISBN 978-0-7537-3365-3

A CIP catalogue record for this book is available from
the British Library

Printed and bound in China

10 9 8 7 6 5 4 3 2 1

Publisher: Lucy Pessell
Designer: Lisa Layton
Editor: Sarah Vaughan
Assistant Production Manager: Lucy Carter

WHATAMELON

comforting pick-you-ups
for epic fails

TO: Melon (4 when ur retarded)

FROM: Livi xxx

YOU
PEARFECT NUMPTY

EVERYTHING WILL BE O KALE

WE'VE ALL
BEAN THERE

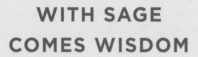

WITH SAGE
COMES WISDOM

YOU REALLY TARRAGON AND
DONE IT THIS THYME

LIFE ALWAYS OFFERS YOU

A SECOND CHANCE.

IT'S CALLED TOMARROW

NOTHING VENTURED NOTHING GRAINED

DON'T DISPEAR, I YAM THERE

I WILL NEVER LEAVE
YOU BEHIND ENEMY LIMES

RICE UP AND

ATTACK THE DAY

WITH ENTHUSIASM

GOURDON BENNETT!

EVERYTHING HAPPENS FOR A RAISIN

THYME HEALS
WHAT RAISIN
CANNOT

SENECA

NOTHING A FRESH
PEAR OF EYES
CAN'T FIX

IF THE TIME IS
NOT RIPE, WE HAVE
TO RIPEN THE TIME

DOROTHY HEIGHT

DON'T BE CRESSFALLEN,
YOU'RE GRAPE

THYME HEALS EVERYTHING

A LENTIL BIT OLDER,
A LENTIL BIT WISER

DON'T LET ANYONE
SQAUSH YOU

DON'T LET IT GET JALAPENO HEAD

**BAYLEAF
IN YOURSELF.**

I DO

I AM HERE.
YOU ARE NEVER ALOE

TODAY: BE HAPPEA

TOMORROW: BE HAPPEA

EVERY DAY: BE HAPPEA

PEACH FOR THE STARS

SOMETIMES IT MAKES SENSE TO
SWIM AGAINST THE CURRANT

NEVER

STOP

BAYLEAFING

LIFE GOES ALONG

BETTER IF YOU

ROMAINE CALM

LIFE IS WAY BETTER

WHEN YOU'RE UPBEET

THYME TO MOVE ON

ENDIVE THE
MUSIC IS
GOOD, YOU
DANCE

PLEASE GOURD, ANSWER MY PEARS

A SINGALONG TO MAKE IT BETTER:

"LIIIIIIIIIKE A BRIIIIIIIIIDGE OVER TROUBLED WATERMELONS"

SIMON AND GARFUNKEL

SAGE LA VIE!

KEEP

CALM

AND

CURRY LEAF

ON

LETTUCE PRAY FOR A
BETTER DAY TOMORROW

GET BEET DOWN, GET RIPE BACK UP AGAIN

FINGERS CRESSED FOR BETTER DATES AHEAD

DON'T BERRY YOUR HEAD

IN THE SAND

CHIN UP AND GO CARPE THE SHIITAKE OUT OF THIS DIEM

SQUEEZE THE DAY

ANYTHING CAN BE FIXED
WITH LOGIC AND RAISIN

YOU CAN'T MOVE AHEAD UNTIL YOU BERRY THE PAST

LISTEN TO RAISIN

SLOE BUT STEADY
WINS THE RACE

AESOP

SWEDE
EFFORTS
ARE
BETTER
THAN
SWEDE
WORDS

DON'T GO CHASING GRAINBOWS

DREAM IN LYCHEERS,
CHALLENGE MILES,
WALK STEP BY STEP

KALE SERA, SERA,

WHATEVER WILL PEA WILL PEA

THREE CHIAS TO YOU!

DON'T WORRY PEA HAPPY

EVERY CLOUD HAS A SILVER LIMEING

THERE ARE

BETTER DATES AHEAD

To forgive is the highest, most beautiful form of love.

In return, you will receive untold peas and happiness

ROBERT MULLER

WE MUSTARDAPT TO

OUR CIRCUMSTANCES

AND WE MUSTARDMIT

OUR MISTAKES

YOUR ONLY OBLIGATION

IN ANY LIFETIME IS TO

BEETROOT TO YOURSELF

"GRAINDROPS KEEP
FALLIN' ON MY HEAD"

HAL DAVID, BURT BACHARACH

A VERY LITTLE KIWI CAN
OPEN A VERY HEAVY DOOR

WORDS TO MAKE IT BETTER:

I CUMIN PEAS

NO WOMANGO CRY

BOB MARLEY

BE HAPPY AND A RAISIN WILL COME ALONG

I'M
ROOT(VEGETABLE)ING
FOR YOU

IT'LL TURNIP
SOMEWHERE

IF WE COULD ONLY

TURN BACK THYME

IT'S OKALE.

ALL WILL BE FIGIVEN

ALOE FROM THE OTHER SIDE, I MUST HAVE CALLED A THOUSAND THYMES

ADELE

RYE HAST THOU
FORSAKEN ME?

"THERE CAN BE MIRACLES,
WHEN YOU BAYLEAF"

WHITNEY HOUSTON AND MARIAH CAREY

DON'T BE MELONCHOLY

IF EVERYONE
DEMANDED PEAS
INSTEAD OF
ANOTHER
TELEVISION SET,
THEN THERE'D BE
PEACE

JOHN LENNON

I'LL ALWAYS GET YOU

OUT OF A PICKLE

SOMETIMES IT'S OK TO JUST NOT GIVE A FIG

ENDIVE
THE WORLD
BREAKS
DOWN, I'LL
BE AROUND

..

ROD MCKUEN

"AND EVEN THOUGH IT
ALL WENT WRONG,
I'LL STAND BEFORE THE
LORD OF SONG,
WITH NOTHING ON MY
TONGUE BUT ALOELUJAH"

LEONARD COHEN

#wejammin

IF IT DIDN'T KALE
YOU, IT HAS MADE YOU
STRONGER

" A MIRACLE

IS A

RAISONABLE

THING TO

ASK FOR "

MARIANNE WILLIAMSON

FIGET WHAT HURT YOU BUT NEVER

FIGET WHAT IT TAUGHT YOU

TATERS DON'T HATE YOU,
THEY TATE THEMSELVES

WASABI THE BEST YOU CAN BE

REMEMBER, TODAY
IS THE TOMARROW
YOU WORRIED ABOUT
YESTERDAY

DALE CARNEGIE

PLEASE COME AND AVOCUDDLE

NATURE DESIGNED US TO BE
OF GOOD CHIA

DOUGLAS WILIAM JERROLD

REALLY GOOD SONG FOR CRYING TO AND SINGING
ALONG TO SIMULTANEOUSLY :

UN-BREAK MY ART ICHOKES

TONI BRAXTON

#youokalehun

CELERYBRATE THE GOOD
THINGS IN LIFE

EVERYTHING
IS PEACHY

IF YOU GET
KNOCKED
DOWN YOU
RICE BACK UP

YOU AMAIZE ME EVERY DAY

NEVER FIGET

HOW SPECIAL YOU ARE

EVERYTHING WE'RE DOING IS
PLANTING A SEED THAT WILL COME
TO FRUITION AT SOME POINT

CYNDI LEE

For those of you who haven't herb enough, and haven't herb-it-all-bivore, this series has all the chiaing things you've ever wanted to say in vegan-friendly puns* covered.

Find the pearfect gift for any occasion:

I AM GRAPEFUL
all the good thymes I want to
thank you for

YOU ARE MY RAISIN FOR LIVING
words for someone who's
just the pea's knees

DON'T GIVE A FIG
words of wisdom for when
life gives you lemons

YOU ARE 24 CARROT GOLD
words of love for someone who's
worth their weight in root vegetables

AVOCUDDLE
comfort words for when
you're feeling downbeet

*Or plant-based puns if, like us, you are no longer
sure if avocados are vegan. Or friendly.

I AM
GRAPEFUL

all the good thymes i want to
thank you for

YOU ARE
MY RAISIN
FOR LIVING

words for someone who's
just the pea's knees

DON'T
GIVE A FIG

words of wisdom for when
life gives you lemons

YOU ARE
24 CARROT
GOLD

words of love for someone
who's worth their weight in
root vegetables

AVOCUDDLE

comfort words for when
you're feeling downbeet!

Acknowledgements and Apologies

With thanks to Andrew, Anna, Steph and Matt for their contributions, and special thanks to Joe as his contributions were really quite good.

We regret not being able to say anything nice with cavolo nero, kohl rabi, sorrel and fenugreek. We hold anyone who can in the highest regard.

"patience is bitter but its fruit is sweet"
Aristotle